The Separate Egg

Egg

○ ○ ○

Recipes for Whites

Pat Field and Pat Kery

St. Martin's Press ○ New York

Design by Laura Hammond Hough

Library of Congress Cataloging in Publication Data

Kery, Patricia Frantz.
    The separate egg.

    1. Cookery (Eggs)   I. Field, Pat.   II. Title.
TX745.K47   1985   641.6′754   85-12527
ISBN 0-312-71303-7 (pbk.)

First Edition
10 9 8 7 6 5 4 3 2 1

Contents

○   ○   ○

Note: The number of egg whites needed in each recipe is indicated by the circled number in the margin.

Introduction and Acknowledgments

○ ○ ○

I learned the value of eggs in Bequia, a tiny island in the Grenadines, where food is scarce and our version of a grocery store is nonexistent. Obtaining groceries from the nearby island of St. Vincent is an all day project and the selection is small.

With such a limited supply of groceries, one learns to be creative in cooking and to use everything available.

Eggs are especially rare and expensive. Therefore, by separating the egg white and yolk, I found one egg has two uses. For instance, to jazz up cheese and crackers as an appetizer, I created a cheddar cheese puff by adding egg whites. A whipped egg white can also add an elegant touch to an otherwise plain dessert like rum pears.

You don't have to be on a remote island to enjoy these fabulous recipes or to appreciate the many, many uses of *The Separate Egg*.

I want to thank all those people who helped with recipes and tested many of the dishes in this book. Thanks to Martha, Pats, Sherri, Bob, George, Thayer, Crispin, Renee, Sheila, Dilys, Luella, and Cindy.

—Pat Field

Appetizers

o o o

Parmesan Croûtes
MAKES 24 CROÛTES

¹/₃ cup mayonnaise
²/₃ cup freshly grated Parmesan cheese
Salt and freshly ground black pepper to taste
1 teaspoon grated lemon rind
6 pinches of curry powder

1 teaspoon dry mustard
2 tablespoons finely chopped onion
¹/₂ teaspoon dry sherry
1 egg white, stiffly beaten
24 bread rounds

Preheat oven to 425°F.

Combine mayonnaise with cheese. Add remaining ingredients, except for the egg white; blend thoroughly. Fold in egg white. Adjust seasoning, if necessary.

Use a teaspoon to mound mixture onto bread rounds. Bake for 10 to 12 minutes, or until rounds are golden brown. Serve hot.

Shrimp Balls

MAKES ABOUT 24 TO 36

2 pounds shrimp, shelled and
   deveined
1 egg white
1 1/2 teaspoons cornstarch

1 tablespoon soy sauce
Salt and freshly ground black
   pepper to taste
Sesame oil for deep-frying

Rinse shrimp in cold water and pat dry. Mince or process to a fine consistency. Mix with egg white, cornstarch, and soy sauce. Shape into balls.

Fry in hot sesame oil for 6 to 8 minutes. Season with additional soy sauce or salt and pepper, if desired, and serve immediately.

Meat Croquettes

SERVES 4

3 tablespoons butter
5 tablespoons all-purpose flour
1 cup beef broth
1 1/2 cups (3/4 pound) ground
   beef, veal, or chicken
1/2 teaspoon salt

Freshly ground black pepper to
   taste
1 teaspoon Worcestershire
   sauce
1 cup fine dry bread crumbs
2 egg whites, lightly beaten
Vegetable oil for deep-frying

Melt butter in a medium saucepan; mix in flour. Add beef broth gradually, stirring constantly until a smooth, thick paste is formed. Add ground meat, salt, pepper, and Worcestershire sauce. Remove from heat. Spread the mixture in an 8-inch square baking dish and chill for 2 hours, until firm.

Cut into 8 equal parts; form each part into a cylinder 3 inches long and 1 inch in diameter. Roll each cylinder in bread crumbs; dip into beaten egg whites and then dredge again in bread crumbs.

Heat oil for deep frying to 375°F. Deep-fry the croquettes for 5 minutes, until the bread crumbs are crisp and brown. Serve piping hot with mustard.

Cold Borscht

SERVES 4

4 cups beef stock or broth
1 bunch beets (5–7), grated
1/2 cup dry red wine
2 tablespoons tomato paste
2 bay leaves

3 egg whites, stiffly beaten
Salt and cayenne pepper to
  taste
4 tablespoons sour cream
Grated rind of 1 lemon

Combine stock, beets, wine, tomato paste, bay leaves, and egg whites in a large saucepan or kettle. Cook, whisking, over medium heat until mixture comes to a boil. Remove from heat; let stand for 10 minutes. Pour soup through a sieve lined with dampened cheesecloth. Place in refrigerator until chilled.

Before serving, season with salt and cayenne pepper. Serve in bowls, topped with sour cream and a sprinkling of grated lemon rind.

Cheddar Cheese Puffs

MAKES ABOUT 40 TO 50 PUFFS

W
H
I
T
E
S

1 loaf Italian bread
6 ounces cream cheese, cut up
1 cup butter, cut up

8 ounces extra-sharp Cheddar
cheese, shredded
1 teaspoon dry mustard
4 egg whites, stiffly beaten

Cut bread into 1-inch slices and cut slices into 1-inch cubes.

In medium saucepan, over low heat, mix together cream cheese, butter, cheddar cheese, and mustard. Remove from heat when well blended; cool slightly. Gently fold in egg whites.

Using a fork, dip bread cubes into cheese mixture, coating evenly on all but one side. Arrange on wax paper–lined trays, uncoated sides down; place in freezer until frozen. Place in plastic bag, seal, and store in freezer until ready to use.

Preheat oven to 400°F. Place frozen puffs, uncoated sides down, on lightly greased cookie sheet. Bake 10 to 12 minutes, or until golden brown. Serve immediately.

Crab Puffs

MAKES 32 PUFFS

1 1/4 cups mayonnaise
1/2 pound cooked crabmeat,
   flaked
1 tablespoon chopped fresh
   chives
1/4 teaspoon freshly ground
   black pepper

1/4 teaspoon cayenne pepper
4 egg whites, at room
   temperature
3/4 teaspoon cream of tartar
16 slices bread
Paprika

Combine mayonnaise, crabmeat, chives, and black and cayenne peppers in a bowl. Set aside.

Beat egg whites in a separate bowl until foamy. Add cream of tartar and beat whites until stiff. Fold the crabmeat mixture into beaten whites and set aside.

Preheat broiler.

Toast bread slices. Trim off crusts and halve slices diagonally. Arrange toast triangles on a large baking sheet. Top each triangle with a heaping tablespoon of the crab mixture; sprinkle with paprika.

Broil 4 to 5 inches from heat source until puffed and golden brown, 3 to 5 minutes. Serve hot.

Entrées

○ ○ ○

① Chicken Quenelles with Lemon Sauce

MAKES 3 DOZEN

QUENELLES

*¹/₂ pound boneless, skinless
chicken breast, ground (in
food processor or with meat
grinder)*
¹/₂ teaspoon salt

*¹/₄ teaspoon freshly ground
black pepper*
¹/₈ teaspoon nutmeg
1 egg white, lightly beaten
1 cup heavy cream

Mix together chicken, salt, pepper, and nutmeg. Mix in egg white. Add cream gradually; stir until mixture is firm enough to hold its shape.

Generously butter a large skillet. Dip 2 teaspoons into boiling water. Heap some of the chicken mixture on one spoon and round it off with second spoon. Dip second spoon into hot water again, slip it under the oval, and slide quenelle into buttered skillet. Repeat procedure until quenelles line the skillet in a single layer; do not crowd. Slowly add enough hot salted water or stock to the skillet to float the quenelles. Bring liquid to a simmer over low heat and poach the quenelles until they are firm, about 5 to 10 minutes; do not allow to boil. Remove quenelles with a slotted spoon and drain well on paper toweling. Keep warm while you make lemon sauce.

LEMON SAUCE

2½ cups chicken broth
3 tablespoons lemon juice
1 tablespoon dried tarragon

½ cup butter, cut into 8 pieces
Salt and freshly ground black
   pepper to taste

Bring chicken broth to a boil in a saucepan. Add lemon juice and tarragon; continue to boil until the liquid is reduced to 1 cup.

Pour liquid into a blender or food processor. With motor running, add butter, one piece at a time. Blend until the sauce is creamy. Season with salt and pepper to taste.

Serve quenelles accompanied by the sauce.

Shrimp Cantonese

SERVES 6 TO 8

W
H
I
T
E

1 pound shrimp, shelled and
   deveined
2 tablespoons plus 1/2 teaspoon
   dry sherry
1 egg white
1/2 teaspoon baking soda
1 teaspoon sesame oil
1/8 teaspoon freshly ground
   black pepper
2 whole scallions, chopped
1 teaspoon minced fresh ginger
2 teaspoons minced garlic

1 teaspoon salted black beans,
   rinsed in hot water, drained,
   and mashed into a paste
1/2 teaspoon granulated sugar
2 teaspoons cornstarch
1 tablespoon dark soy sauce
2 teaspoons light soy sauce
1/2 cup chicken stock or broth
6 tablespoons vegetable oil
1/4 pound minced pork
1/2 green or red bell pepper,
   cored, peeled, and cut into
   1-inch pieces
2 eggs, lightly beaten

Rinse shrimp in cold water and pat dry. Mix with the ½ teaspoon sherry, egg white, baking soda, ½ teaspoon of the sesame oil, and black pepper. Refrigerate at least 1 hour.

Mix together scallions, ginger, garlic, and beans; set aside.

Mix together sugar, cornstarch, soy sauce, remaining ½ teaspoon sesame oil, chicken broth, and the 2 tablespoons sherry. Set sauce aside.

Place a wok over high heat. Swirl in 4 tablespoons of the vegetable oil. When oil is hot, add shrimp mixture and stir-fry until shrimp just turn pink-white, less than 1 minute. Remove with slotted spoon to bowl. Wipe wok clean.

Place wok over high heat. Swirl in remaining 2 tablespoons vegetable oil. Add scallion mixture. Stir-fry until garlic turns golden. Add pork. When pork loses pink color, mix in green or red pepper. Add sauce mixture, stirring constantly. When sauce begins to boil, return shrimp to wok and toss well.

Pour eggs over shrimp mixture; do not stir. Reduce heat to medium, cover wok, and cook until eggs are slightly set around the edge, about 2 minutes. Stir to mix well. Serve immediately.

Broccoli Soufflé
SERVES 6

W
H
I
T
E

3 tablespoons butter
3 tablespoons all-purpose flour
1 cup milk
1 cup freshly grated Parmesan
   cheese
Salt and freshly ground black
   pepper to taste

3 egg yolks
1 cup cooked broccoli, passed
   through a food mill (see note
   below)
4 egg whites
Hollandaise Sauce (see Yolks,
   page 36)

Preheat oven to 350°F.

Melt butter in a saucepan over medium heat. Add flour and cook 2 minutes, stirring constantly. Add milk gradually, whisking until mixture is thickened; stir in cheese and seasonings. Remove from heat and let cool slightly.

Whisk in the yolks, one at a time. Stir in the broccoli purée.

Beat egg whites until stiff and fold into cooled mixture. Pour into a buttered 1½-quart soufflé dish and bake for 45 minutes until soufflé has risen and is firm and brown on top. Serve immediately, accompanied by the Hollandaise Sauce, if desired.

NOTE: Any puréed vegetable can be substituted for the broccoli.

Chicken-Cognac Soufflé

SERVES 4 TO 6

3 tablespoons butter
3 tablespoons all-purpose flour
1 cup chicken broth
3 egg yolks
1 cup chopped, cooked chicken
2 tablespoons Cognac
Salt and freshly ground pepper
   to taste

Dash of cayenne pepper
Juice of 1/2 lemon
Pinch of freshly grated nutmeg
1/4 teaspoon dried rosemary
5 egg whites
1/8 teaspoon cream of tartar
Velouté Sauce (see Yolks, page
   31)

Preheat oven to 400°F. Butter a 1-quart soufflé dish.

Melt butter in a medium saucepan; blend in flour. Add chicken broth gradually, stirring with a whisk to form a thick, smooth sauce. Remove pan from the heat, let cool slightly, then add yolks, one at a time. Mix in the chicken, Cognac, salt, pepper, cayenne, lemon juice, nutmeg, and rosemary.

Beat egg whites in a large bowl with a pinch of salt and the cream of tartar. Fold chicken mixture into egg whites. Pour mixture into prepared soufflé dish.

Place soufflé dish in oven and reduce temperature to 375°F. Bake soufflé for 25 minutes. Serve with Velouté Sauce.

Shrimp or Crab Soufflé with Avocado

SERVES 4 TO 6

W
H
I
T
E
S

3 tablespoons butter
$1/4$ cup all-purpose flour
$1^1/2$ cups milk or chicken broth
6 egg yolks
1 cup chopped, cooked shrimp, shelled and deveined, or crabmeat
1 teaspoon tomato paste

1 avocado, thinly sliced and sprinkled with juice of $1/2$ lime or lemon
Salt and freshly ground black pepper to taste
$1/8$ teaspoon cream of tartar
8 egg whites

Preheat oven to 400°F. Butter a 2-quart soufflé dish.

Melt butter in a medium saucepan; blend in flour. Stir in milk or chicken broth gradually to make a thick, smooth sauce. Remove pan from heat, let cool slightly, then add yolks, one at a time. Stir in the shellfish, tomato paste, avocado, and seasonings.

Add a pinch of salt and cream of tartar to the egg whites in a large bowl and beat until stiff. Fold shellfish mixture into whites; pour into prepared soufflé dish.

Place soufflé dish in the oven and reduce temperature to 375°F. Bake soufflé for 25 minutes. Serve immediately.

Mile-High Cheese Soufflé

SERVES 6

1/2 cup butter or margarine
1/2 cup all-purpose flour
1 teaspoon salt
Pinch of freshly ground black
  pepper
2 cups milk

2 cups (about 1/2 pound)
  shredded sharp Cheddar
  cheese
8 egg yolks
10 egg whites

Preheat oven to 475°F. Generously butter a 2 1/2-quart soufflé dish or casserole.

Melt butter or margarine in heavy saucepan over medium heat; stir in flour, salt, and pepper. Add milk and cook over low heat until sauce is thickened and smooth, stirring constantly. Add cheese and continue to stir until it melts. Remove from heat.

Beat yolks until light. Gradually add to sauce in fine stream, beating constantly.

Beat egg whites in large bowl until stiff. Gently fold cheese sauce into whites; pour into prepared soufflé dish. To form "top hat," run tip of knife around dish 1 inch from edge.

Bake soufflé for 10 minutes at 475°F. Reduce temperature to 400°F and bake an additional 25 to 30 minutes, until puffed and brown. Serve immediately.

Lobster Soufflé

SERVES 4 TO 6

3 WHITES

3 tablespoons butter
¼ cup chopped shallots
¼ cup all-purpose flour
1 cup fish or chicken stock
¼ cup heavy cream
6 egg yolks
1 tablespoon tomato paste
2 tablespoons Cognac

1 cup cooked lobster meat
Salt and freshly ground black
  pepper to taste
9 egg whites
⅛ teaspoon cream of tartar
¼ cup freshly grated Parmesan
  cheese

Preheat oven to 400°F. Butter a 1½-quart soufflé dish.

Melt butter in a medium saucepan; add shallots and sauté until softened. Stir in flour. Gradually add chicken or fish stock and cream, stirring constantly to thicken and smooth the sauce. Remove from heat and add yolks, one at a time. Stir in tomato paste, Cognac, lobster meat, and salt and pepper.

Add a pinch of salt and the cream of tartar to the egg whites in a large bowl and beat until stiff. Fold lobster mixture into beaten whites. Pour into prepared soufflé dish; sprinkle with Parmesan cheese.

Place soufflé dish in oven and reduce temperature to 375°F. Bake soufflé for 25 minutes. Serve immediately.

Oyster and Bacon Soufflé

SERVES 4 TO 6

3 tablespoons butter
¹/4 cup all-purpose flour
1 pint oysters, drained and
   liquid reserved
6 egg yolks

8 strips bacon, fried until crisp,
   drained, and crumbled
Dash of cayenne pepper
Salt to taste
9 egg whites
¹/8 teaspoon cream of tartar

Preheat oven to 400°F. Butter a 1¹/2-quart soufflé dish.

Melt butter in a medium saucepan; blend in the flour. Add enough milk to reserved oyster liquid to measure 1 cup; add combined oyster liquid and milk gradually to saucepan, stirring constantly with a whisk. Remove from heat; add yolks, one at a time. Fold in the oysters, bacon, cayenne pepper, and salt to taste.

Add a pinch of salt and the cream of tartar to egg whites in a large bowl; beat until stiff. Fold the oyster/bacon mixture into beaten whites; pour into prepared soufflé dish.

Place soufflé dish in oven and reduce temperature to 375°F. Bake soufflé for 25 minutes. Serve immediately.

Veal Almondine

SERVES 6

6 veal scallops (4 to 6 ounces
 each)
Salt and freshly ground black
 pepper to taste
2¹/₂ cups fine dry bread crumbs
1¹/₂ cups lightly toasted sliced,
 blanched almonds

¹/₃ cup minced fresh parsley
3 tablespoons grated lemon
 rind
3 egg whites
³/₄ cup butter or margarine
2 lemons, sliced
Lemon juice (optional)

Pound veal scallops until they are ¹/₄ inch thick. Season with salt
and pepper.

In a shallow bowl, combine bread crumbs, almonds, parsley,
and lemon rind. In another shallow bowl, beat egg whites lightly.

Dip veal scallops into egg whites, then dredge them in the bread-
crumb mixture. Place scallops on a baking sheet and chill for at
least 30 minutes.

Melt butter over medium heat in a large skillet. Add veal and
sauté for 1 to 2 minutes per side, until golden and just cooked.
Transfer to a heated platter and garnish with lemon slices.
Squeeze lemon juice over veal, if desired.

NOTE: The scallops may be frozen after cooking. To reheat, place
in a 350°F oven until warmed through, about 20 to 30 minutes.

Desserts, Frostings, and Toppings

o o o

Banana Sherbet

MAKES 2 QUARTS

1 cup granulated sugar
1 cup water
2 cups orange juice

2 tablespoons lemon juice
6 ripe bananas, mashed
1 egg white, lightly beaten

①
W
H
I
T
E

Combine sugar and water in a saucepan over medium heat. Cook, stirring, until sugar has completely dissolved. Stir in orange and lemon juices. Add banana pulp; blend well. Remove from heat and transfer to bowl. Let cool, then place in freezer.

Remove from freezer when mixture is mushy in consistency. Fold in egg white. Return to freezer and cover. Serve when firm.

Memphis Lemon Meringue Whip

SERVES 8 TO 10

WHITE

5 egg whites
1/4 teaspoon cream of tartar
1 1/2 cups granulated sugar
4 egg yolks

Grated rind of 1 lemon
2 tablespoons lemon juice
1/2 pint heavy cream

Preheat oven to 250°F. Butter a round cake pan.

Beat egg whites until frothy. Add cream of tartar and beat until stiff. Gradually add 1 cup of the sugar, beating until mixture is somewhat glossy.

Turn mixture into prepared cake pan and bake for 1 hour. Carefully remove meringue from pan and transfer to a plate. Let cool.

Beat yolks until light in top of double boiler; stir in lemon rind, lemon juice, and remaining 1/2 cup sugar. Cook over simmering water, stirring constantly, until mixture has thickened. Remove from heat and let cool.

Beat heavy cream until stiff. Spread half the whipped cream over meringue shell. Top with cooled custard mixture; finish with remaining whipped cream.

Carefully cover top and sides of dessert with wax paper. Refrigerate overnight before serving.

Soufflé Rothschild
SERVES 6 TO 8

2 tablespoons kirsch
3/4 cup chopped glacéed fruits
3 tablespoons butter
3 tablespoons all-purpose flour
1 cup milk
1/2 cup granulated sugar

4 egg yolks
1 teaspoon vanilla
5 egg whites
Pinch of salt
1/8 teaspoon cream of tartar

Preheat oven to 400°F. Butter and sugar a 1-quart soufflé dish.

Add kirsch to chopped fruits and let stand for 5 minutes.

Melt butter in a saucepan, blend in flour. Stir in milk gradually to form a thick, smooth sauce. Stir in sugar. Remove from heat.

Beat in yolks, one at a time. Stir in vanilla and glacéed fruits.

Add a pinch of salt and the cream of tartar to egg whites in large bowl; beat until stiff.

Fold fruit mixture into beaten whites; pour into prepared soufflé dish.

Place soufflé dish in oven and reduce temperature to 375°F. Bake soufflé for 20 minutes. Serve immediately, accompanied by whipped cream.

Sugared Nuts

MAKES 1 POUND

1 cup granulated sugar
1 teaspoon ground cinnamon
1/2 teaspoon nutmeg
1/4 teaspoon salt

1 egg white
1 tablespoon water
1 pound pecan halves, almonds, or walnuts

Preheat oven to 275°F.

Mix sugar, cinnamon, nutmeg, and salt in small bowl. Set aside. Beat egg white with water in large bowl; stir in nuts to coat well. Dip nuts in sugar mixture until well coated. Transfer to greased cookie sheet and bake for 1 hour, stirring every 10 minutes. Let cool.

Coffee Liqueur Mousse

MAKES 10 TO 12 SERVINGS

6 tablespoons butter, cut up
1 pound dark sweet chocolate, cut up
1/2 cup sifted confectioners sugar
3 egg yolks
1/4 cup coffee liqueur

1 teaspoon instant coffee powder, preferably espresso
2 cups heavy cream, stiffly beaten
4 egg whites, beaten until soft peaks form
Chocolate shavings (optional)

Melt butter and chocolate in top of double boiler over simmering water. Let cool.

Mix together sugar, yolks, coffee liqueur, and instant coffee in a large bowl; stir in cooled chocolate mixture. Gently fold in first the whipped cream, then the beaten whites. Refrigerate mousse overnight.

To serve, spoon into individual dessert dishes or one bowl. Garnish with chocolate shavings, if desired.

Derek's Key Lime Pie

SERVES 6 TO 8

This pie owes its distinctive flavor to the key lime, a native citrus of Florida. The key lime is smaller in size than the average store-bought lime and is noticeably sweeter.

3 egg yolks
1 can (15 ounces) sweetened condensed milk
6 tablespoons lime juice, preferably key lime

1 tablespoon finely grated lime rind
One 9-inch graham cracker crust
4 egg whites
3 cups granulated sugar

Preheat oven to 350°F.

Beat together egg yolks, condensed milk, lime juice, and lime rind. If using regular limes, add 1 teaspoon more sugar. Pour into prepared crust.

Beat egg whites in large bowl until foamy; gradually beat in sugar until stiff. Spoon meringue over lime mixture, spreading it to touch edges of crust.

Bake for 10 to 15 minutes. Let cool before serving.

Fluffy Brown Sugar Frosting

2 WHITES

MAKES ENOUGH TO FROST AN 8- OR 9-INCH
LAYER CAKE OR A 13- x 9-INCH SHEET CAKE

*1 1/2 cups firmly packed brown
   sugar*
1/3 cup water

2 egg whites
1 teaspoon vanilla

Mix together all ingredients in top of double boiler over simmering water. Beat with an electric mixer for 7 minutes, or until soft peaks form. Remove from heat and let cool before using.

Fluffy Butter Icing

2 WHITES

MAKES ENOUGH TO FROST AN
8- OR 9-INCH LAYER CAKE

4 tablespoons butter
1 1/2 cups confectioners sugar

2 egg whites

Cream butter until light. Gradually add 1/2 cup of the sugar; set aside.

Beat egg whites until foamy. Gradually add remaining 1 cup sugar and beat until stiff. Add creamed mixture and blend well.

Rum Pears

SERVES 10

*3/4 cup plus 3 tablespoons
   granulated sugar*
3 tablespoons apricot jam
1/2 cup water
Few drops of lemon juice
*5 pears, peeled, halved, and
   cored*
1 egg

1 egg yolk
3 tablespoons all-purpose flour
2 teaspoons unflavored gelatin
3/4 cup hot milk
3 egg whites, stiffly beaten
2 tablespoons heavy cream
Rum to taste

Combine the 3/4 cup sugar, jam, water, and lemon juice in saucepan over low heat; cook to a thin syrup. Add pears and simmer gently, covered, for 7 to 8 minutes. Remove pears with slotted spoon to serving dish to cool, arranging cut side up; reserve syrup.

Mix together egg, yolk, the 3 tablespoons sugar, and flour in saucepan; beat well. Add gelatin and milk. Cook, stirring, over medium heat just to the boiling point. Remove from heat and stir over ice until cold. Fold in egg whites, cream, and rum. Spoon this mixture into pastry bag fitted with a decorative tip and use to fill pear halves. Top pears with syrup and serve.

White Chocolate Mousse

SERVES 6

WHITES

2 bars (3 ounces each) Swiss
   white chocolate
1/3 cup warm milk
2 egg whites, stiffly beaten

1 cup heavy cream, whipped
Few drops of lemon juice
Dark chocolate curls or
   shavings

Melt chocolate in top of double boiler over simmering water, stirring occasionally. Stir in milk, blending until smooth. Remove from heat and let cool to room temperature.

Fold stiffly beaten egg whites into chocolate with spatula until blended; fold in whipped cream, then lemon juice.

Spoon mixture into 1-quart soufflé dish or glass bowl (individual ramekins or martini glasses may also be used). Swirl top(s) with back of spoon and garnish with chocolate curls or shavings. Cover and chill at least 2 hours.

NOTE: Can be prepared 1 day in advance.

Cream Cheese Fruit Pie

SERVES 6 TO 8

1 1/3 cups (one 15-ounce can)
sweetened condensed milk
1/4 cup lemon juice
6 tablespoons cream cheese,
softened at room temperature
2 egg yolks
1 prebaked 9-inch pie shell

1 cup fruit (sliced fresh
strawberries or raspberries,
or canned crushed pineapple
or pitted tart cherries, well
drained)
4 egg whites
1/4 teaspoon cream of tartar
1/2 cup granulated sugar

Preheat oven to 325°F.

In a large bowl, blend together the condensed milk and lemon juice until thickened.

Beat cream cheese until smooth in a medium bowl. Beat in yolks, one at a time; stir in fruit. Fold this mixture into condensed milk mixture. Pour into prepared pie shell.

Beat egg whites and cream of tartar in a small bowl until whites hold a soft peak. Gradually beat in the sugar; continue to beat just until whites hold firm peaks. Spoon meringue over pie filling, spreading to inside edge of pie shell.

Bake until meringue is golden brown, about 15 minutes. Cool pie to room temperature, then refrigerate until chilled before serving.

Cherry Flan Tart

②

W
H
I
T
E
S

CHERRIES

3 cups pitted Bing cherries
Granulated sugar to taste

Juice of ¹/₂ lemon
¹/₃ cup sweet Port wine

CUSTARD

2 whole eggs
2 egg yolks
1 cup heavy cream

¹/₃ cup granulated sugar
1 teaspoon vanilla
1 teaspoon grated lemon rind

MERINGUE

4 egg whites
Pinch of salt

¹/₂ cup granulated sugar

1 9-inch tart shell, prebaked in
  tart pan with removable sides

Preheat the oven to 350°F.

Place cherries in a bowl, sprinkle with sugar, lemon juice, and Port and let marinate for 30 minutes to 1 hour.

In another bowl, combine whole eggs with yolks, cream, sugar, vanilla, and lemon rind and whisk until mixture is very well blended.

Drain the cherries thoroughly and arrange in the baked tart shell. Top them with custard mixture. Bake tart until the custard is set, 30 to 40 minutes.

Meanwhile, combine egg whites with salt in large bowl and beat, adding the sugar a little at a time, until meringue is stiff and glossy.

Remove tart from oven; increase temperature to 450°F. Spoon meringue over tart filling, covering it completely. Return tart to the oven for 3 or 4 minutes, until meringue is lightly browned. Remove and let cool.

When ready to serve, carefully unmold tart and slide it onto a serving platter.

Chilled Strawberry Soufflé

SERVES 4

W
H
I
T
E
S

1/3 cup granulated sugar
1 envelope unflavored gelatin
1 tablespoon lemon juice
1/2 cup water
1 1/2 cups puréed strawberries
(2 pints fresh strawberries,
hulled, or 1 1/2 packages
frozen)

2 egg whites
1/8 teaspoon salt
1/2 cup heavy cream, whipped
Fresh strawberries (optional)

Combine sugar and gelatin in a small saucepan. Add lemon juice and water. Stir over low heat until gelatin dissolves, about 3 minutes. Remove from heat; stir in puréed strawberries. Chill mixture, stirring occasionally until slightly firm.

Beat egg whites with salt in a large bowl until stiff. Fold in strawberry mixture, then whipped cream.

Pour mixture into a 1-quart soufflé dish or individual dessert dishes. Chill 4 hours.

Garnish with fresh strawberry halves, if desired.

Seven-Minute Frosting

MAKES ENOUGH TO FROST AN
8- OR 9-INCH LAYER CAKE

1 cup granulated sugar
1/2 cup cold water
1/2 teaspoon light corn syrup
3 large egg whites
Pinch of salt

1/4 teaspoon lemon juice
2 tablespoons confectioners
  sugar (optional)
1 teaspoon vanilla

Combine sugar, water, and corn syrup in a small saucepan. Cook over medium heat, stirring constantly, until sugar is dissolved and mixture starts to boil. At that point, stop stirring and let mixture simmer until it reaches 242°F on a candy thermometer or until a few drops in cold water make a firm-soft ball.

When this syrup is almost ready, combine the egg whites, salt, and lemon juice in a mixing bowl and whip until stiff but not dry. (If whites are ready for use before syrup is done, add 2 tablespoons confectioners sugar, which will help to stabilize them. Continue to beat whites on a low speed. If the syrup is ready before the whites—which is preferred—set pan into cold water to stop its cooking and then reheat when ready to use.)

Gradually pour hot syrup over stiff whites; beat mixture until cool. Flavor with vanilla.

Lemon-Orange Soufflé with Fruit Sauce

SERVES 4 TO 6

SOUFFLÉ

4 tablespoons butter or
   margarine
1/4 teaspoon salt
1/3 cup all-purpose flour
1 cup milk
3 egg yolks

3/4 cup granulated sugar
1/4 cup orange juice
1 tablespoon grated orange rind
1 1/2 teaspoons grated lemon
   rind
6 egg whites

Preheat oven to 325°F. Butter a 1½-quart soufflé dish or casserole.

Melt butter or margarine in a heavy saucepan over medium heat; stir in the salt and flour. Reduce heat to low and add milk, stirring constantly until mixture thickens. Remove from heat.

Beat egg yolks in a bowl. Gradually add sugar and beat constantly until mixture is light and fluffy. Stir in the juice and rinds. Combine this mixture with white sauce.

Beat the egg whites in separate bowl until they hold soft peaks; carefully fold into yolk mixture. Pour mixture into prepared soufflé dish; place dish in a pan of hot water. Bake soufflé for 1 hour.

FRUIT SAUCE

2 eggs, separated
1/2 cup sugar
1/4 cup orange juice
1/4 cup lemon juice
1 1/2 teaspoons grated orange
    rind

1/2 teaspoon grated lemon rind
1/8 teaspoon salt
1/4 cup fruit (raspberries or
    strawberries are
    recommended)

Meanwhile, make fruit sauce.

Beat egg yolks and sugar in a saucepan until light and fluffy. Stir in orange and lemon juices and rind, and salt. Cook over low heat until thickened, stirring often.

Beat egg whites until they hold soft peaks; fold yolk mixture into beaten whites. Fold in fruit just prior to serving.

When soufflé is puffed and brown, remove from oven. Serve immediately, accompanied by the sauce.

Tuiles

MAKES 24 COOKIES

2¹/₄ cups sliced blanched
   almonds
³/₄ cup granulated sugar

¹/₄ cup all-purpose flour
3 egg whites
¹/₄ cup melted unsalted butter

Mix together almonds, sugar, and flour in a bowl. Add egg whites and butter; blend thoroughly. Cover and refrigerate at least 1 hour.

Preheat oven to 350°F. Line a baking sheet with foil and butter generously.

Drop the batter by level tablespoonfuls onto prepared baking sheet, leaving 5 to 6 inches between each cookie. Press each mound of batter to an even thickness with a spoon or fork. Bake 12 to 15 minutes, until cookies are deep brown around the edges and firm in the center.

Remove from oven and let stand on baking sheet 30 seconds. Carefully lift each cookie off foil, using a spatula. Invert cookie and curl it around a rolling pin or wine bottle. Repeat process for each cookie. If cookies become too firm to curl, return briefly to oven.

Store cookies in an airtight container in a cool, dry place.

Pecan Cookies

MAKES 36 COOKIES

3 egg whites
¹/₈ teaspoon salt
¹/₂ teaspoon cream of tartar

³/₄ cup granulated sugar
2 cups chopped pecans

Preheat oven to 200°F. Lightly butter and dust with flour a sheet of wax paper placed on a cookie sheet.

Beat egg whites until foamy; add salt and cream of tartar and beat until stiff. Gradually stir in sugar; fold in nuts.

Drop batter by teaspoonfuls onto prepared cookie sheet, spacing them about 1 inch apart. Bake for 1 hour to 1 hour 15 minutes. Remove from oven and let cool, then carefully peel the cookies off the wax paper.

Pistachio Parfait
SERVES 4 TO 6

1 cup granulated sugar
$^1/_3$ cup water
3 egg whites, stiffly beaten
2 teaspoons vanilla

2 cups heavy cream, whipped
1 cup pistachio nuts, coarsely
  ground

Boil the sugar and water in saucepan until syrup spins a light thread, or registers 228°F on a candy thermometer. Pour hot syrup in a fine stream into the stiffly beaten egg whites, beating constantly; continue to beat until meringue is cool. Stir in vanilla. Fold in whipped cream and pistachio nuts, and freeze without stirring in stemmed glasses.

Meringue Nests

MAKES 6 TO 8 NESTS

3
W
H
I
T
E
S

3 egg whites, at room
   temperature
Pinch of salt

1 cup granulated sugar
1/2 teaspoon vinegar
1/2 teaspoon vanilla

Preheat oven to 225°F.

Beat egg whites with salt until foamy. Add sugar, 2 tablespoons at a time. Continue beating until mixture stands in stiff peaks. Add vinegar and vanilla and beat well.

Using a spoon or a pastry tube, shape the meringue into uniform rounds on unglazed paper or a foil-lined cookie sheet.

Bake for 1 hour. Let cool before removing from paper. Top with Chocolate Filling, garnish with whipped cream, chocolate curls, and toasted nuts.

NOTE: Nests may be filled with any sweet custard and are excellent filled with fresh fruit.

CHOCOLATE FILLING

MAKES ABOUT 3/4 CUP

1 1/2 tablespoons all-purpose
   flour
1/2 cup granulated sugar
1/2 teaspoon unsweetened cocoa
   powder

Pinch of salt
1/2 cup milk
2 egg yolks, beaten
1/2 tablespoon butter
1 1/2 teaspoons vanilla

GARNISH

Whipped cream *Toasted nuts*
Chocolate curls

Mix flour, sugar, cocoa, and salt in top of a double boiler. Add half the milk, the beaten yolks, then remaining milk. Cook until thickened. Remove from heat.

Add butter and vanilla to saucepan; beat until creamy. Cool in refrigerator, covering mixture so a crust does not form. Use to fill Meringue Nests.

Baked Alaska
SERVES 8 TO 10

④
W
H
I
T
E
S

Sponge cake *$1/2$ cup granulated sugar*
4 egg whites *1 quart ice cream (any flavor)*
$1/8$ teaspoon cream of tartar *$1/4$ cup Cognac (optional)*

Preheat oven to 450°F. Select a board that will fit in oven. Wet on both sides and shake off excess water. Put pieces of brown paper on top of board and place cake on it.

Beat together egg whites and cream of tartar until foamy. Slowly add sugar and beat just until stiff.

Cut ice cream in slices to cover cake, leaving ½-inch rim all around. Cover with meringue.

Place in oven to brown lightly, about 5 minutes. Serve immediately. For a special touch, warm the Cognac, put match to it to flame, and pour over Baked Alaska.

Silver Cake

WHITES

2³/₄ cups sifted cake flour	1¹/₃ cups milk
1²/₃ cups granulated sugar	²/₃ cup vegetable shortening
4¹/₂ teaspoons baking powder	5 egg whites
1 teaspoon salt	1 teaspoon vanilla

Preheat oven to 350°F. Grease and flour two 8- or 9-inch round layer pans or a 13 × 9-inch sheet pan.

Mix together flour, sugar, baking powder, and salt in a mixing bowl. Add 1 cup of the milk and the shortening; beat vigorously, 300 strokes by hand or at medium speed with an electric mixer for 2 minutes. Add egg whites, remaining ¹/₃ cup milk, and vanilla; beat 300 strokes or 2 minutes more.

Pour batter into prepared pans and bake 35 minutes for the layer cake or 35 to 40 minutes for the sheet cake. Cool 15 minutes before removing cake from pan or pans. Frost with favorite topping.

Sweet Layered Strawberries

SERVES 10 TO 12

WHITES

2 cups whole blanched almonds	1 cup confectioners sugar
1¹/₂ cups plus 5 tablespoons granulated sugar	4 teaspoons hot milk
6 egg whites	2 teaspoons instant coffee powder
1 quart fresh strawberries, washed and hulled	³/₄ teaspoon vanilla
	1 cup heavy cream

Preheat oven to 300°F.

Line two baking sheets with parchment paper. Trace a 10-inch circle on each sheet; do not cut out.

Grind 1 1/2 cups of the almonds and the 1 1/2 cups granulated sugar together in a food processor or blender until very fine.

Beat egg whites until stiff. Gently fold in almond-sugar mixture. Spread onto paper circles. Bake 1 hour. Remove baking sheets from oven; increase oven temperature to 350°F.

Remove meringues from baking sheets, carefully peeling off paper; cool on a rack.

Spread remaining 1/2 cup almonds on a baking sheet and toast until lightly browned, 7 to 8 minutes. Remove from oven and let cool. Grind cooled almonds in a food processor or blender until coarse. Reserve.

Reserving 4 strawberries, halve remaining strawberries and place in a bowl. Sprinkle with 2 tablespoons granulated sugar and mix gently.

In another bowl combine confectioners sugar, hot milk, coffee powder, and 1/2 teaspoon of the vanilla. Mix until smooth. Spread icing on one meringue layer, coating top and sides well.

Beat cream until stiff. Add the remaining 3 tablespoons granulated sugar and remaining 1/4 teaspoon vanilla. Spread on the second meringue layer, coating top and sides. Arrange the strawberries, cut side up, on the cream. Place the iced meringue layer on top. Spread the ground almonds around the sides, pressing into the whipped cream and icing. Arrange the reserved 4 strawberries on top. Refrigerate until serving.

Jamie's Dacquoise

SERVES 8

6 egg whites
Scant 1/2 teaspoon cream of
    tartar
1 teaspoon almond extract
Pinch of salt
2 1/4 cups granulated sugar
2/3 cup cornstarch
1/2 cup finely ground toasted
    almonds, plus additional for
    garnish, if desired

5 eggs
2 cups (1 pound) unsalted
    butter, softened but cool, cut
    into tablespoon-size pieces
1 tablespoon instant espresso
    coffee
2 tablespoons Cognac
1/2 pound semisweet chocolate

Line two cookie sheets with parchment paper. On the parchment, draw three circles about 7 inches in diameter, one on one cookie sheet and two on the other, leaving a space between the latter two.

Preheat oven to 300°F.

Beat egg whites with cream of tartar, almond extract, and salt until soft peaks form. Continuing to beat at high speed, add 1 cup of the sugar, a tablespoon at a time. Beat until whites are dry and stiff.

In a separate bowl, mix together 1/2 cup of the sugar, the cornstarch, and 1/2 cup ground nuts; fold gently into the meringue.

To make the top of the dacquoise, use a pastry bag and a plain round tip (no. 7, or 5/8 inch in diameter) and pipe concentric circles of meringue (about ½ inch thick) to fill in one of the drawn circles. Fill in where necessary. Pipe another layer of meringue directly on top of first, but starting ½ inch in toward center of circle. Repeat a third time, ½ inch in, to complete top layer of dacquoise, forming a pyramid shape.

Using a spatula or the pastry bag, fill in the remaining two circle shapes with one layer of meringue each, each slightly less than ½ inch thick. If desired, pipe any extra meringue in strands on cookie sheet to use for decoration later.

Bake at 300°F until just slightly stiff and dry—at least 2½ hours. Turn off oven and leave meringue in overnight or until cooled. Remove from paper.

To make buttercream filling, beat eggs and remaining ¾ cup sugar over low heat until sugar dissolves. Remove from heat and beat with a mixer until completely cooled. Lower speed and beat in butter, piece by piece, until light and fluffy.

Dissolve espresso in Cognac and add to egg mixture; beat well.

Melt chocolate in top of double boiler.

To assemble: Spread the two flat layers of meringue with chocolate, then generous layers of buttercream filling. Place one on top of the other. Place the top, triple-layer meringue on last. Cover sides with buttercream and use either additional ground almonds or extra meringue, crushed, as garnish over the buttercream.

Lady Baltimore Cake

³/₄ cup butter
1¹/₂ cups granulated sugar
3 cups sifted cake flour
3 teaspoons baking powder
¹/₄ teaspoon salt

1 cup milk
1 teaspoon vanilla
¹/₂ teaspoon almond, rum, or
  brandy extract
6 egg whites, beaten stiff

Preheat oven to 350°F. Grease and dust with flour three 8- or 9-inch round cake pans.

With electric mixer, cream butter until fluffy. Slowly add sugar and continue to mix until mixture is like whipped cream.

Sift flour with baking powder and salt. Alternately add flour and milk to creamed mixture. Add flavorings and mix until smooth. Fold in beaten egg whites with rubber spatula.

Turn batter into prepared pans and bake for 25 minutes. Let cool for 5 minutes in pan before turning onto cooling rack. Frost as desired when thoroughly cooled.

Iced Lemon Mousse
SERVES 8

1 package unflavored gelatin
1 tablespoon water
$^1/_2$ cup lemon juice
1 cup granulated sugar
Grated rind of 1 lemon

7 egg whites
1 cup heavy cream
4 paper-thin lemon slices and 4
    mint leaves or whipped
    cream (optional)

Mix together gelatin and water in small saucepan. Add lemon juice and sugar. Stir over low flame until gelatin is completely dissolved. Add lemon rind.

Refrigerate until mixture is cooled and has syrupy consistency.

Beat egg whites until stiff. Beat in lemon mixture.

Whip cream until stiff. Gently fold into lemon mixture.

Pour mousse mixture into 2-quart bowl and chill at least 4 hours.

To serve, decorate with lemon slices and mint leaves or dollops of whipped cream.

Luis' Angel Food Cake

SERVES 10 TO 12

W
H
I
T
E
S

1 cup all-purpose flour, sifted
1/2 cup confectioners sugar (see
   note below)
10 egg whites (see note below)
2 1/2 tablespoons cold water

1 1/2 teaspoons cream of tartar
1/4 teaspoon vanilla
1 teaspoon almond extract
1/2 teaspoon salt
1 cup granulated sugar

Preheat oven to 350°F. Sift together flour and confectioners sugar. Resift 5 times.

In separate bowl, combine egg whites, water, cream of tartar, vanilla, almond extract, and salt. Beat with electric mixer until eggs are foamy. Gradually add granulated sugar, about 2 tablespoons at a time. Continue to beat until eggs are stiff but not dry.

Stir in flour mixture. Transfer batter to ungreased 10-inch tube pan (see note below). Bake approximately 45 minutes.

Remove tube pan from oven. To cool, invert tube pan on bottle or inverted funnel. Let sit about 1 1/2 hours. Unmold and dust with confectioners sugar.

NOTES: Use egg whites that are at least 3 days old and have been brought to room temperature. Make sure pan is completely grease free; otherwise cake will not rise. If beating egg whites by hand, substitute granulated sugar for confectioners sugar to sift with flour, and use only 1/4 cup.

Egg Shells

○   ○   ○

Camper's Coffee

①
S
H
E
L
L

Regular-grind coffee
1 whole egg (up to 10 cups coffee)

Cold water
Pinch of salt

For each cup, measure 2 tablespoons of coffee into a saucepan or old-fashioned coffee pot. Crack egg into pot and add crushed shell. For each cup you make, add 1 cup cold water. Add a pinch of salt and cover.

Bring coffee just to boil and remove from heat. Sprinkle with a little cold water and let settle a few minutes before pouring.

The egg shell helps the grounds to settle.

Geranium Fertilizer

②
S
H
E
L
L
S

Place 2 egg shells in a quart jar. Fill with water. Let stand a couple days at room temperature. Use this water once a week on your geranium house plants.

Beef Consommé

MAKES ABOUT 10 CUPS

3

S
H
E
L
L
S

1¹/₂ pounds lean shin or shank
    of beef, cut into small pieces
    or minced
10 cups beef stock
Salt and freshly ground black
    pepper to taste
1 onion, chopped

1 carrot, chopped
1 bay leaf
3 egg whites and shells
²/₃ cup dark cream sherry
Beef extract or beef bouillon
    cube (optional)

Place meat in saucepan or kettle with stock. Bring just to boiling point. Add salt, pepper, onion, carrot, and bay leaf. Simmer for 30 minutes.

Add egg shells and lightly whisked egg whites. Simmer gently another 30 minutes. Remove from heat and strain through several layers of cheesecloth or muslin.

Reheat, adding sherry. If consommé is not sufficiently dark, add a very small amount of beef extract or beef bouillon cube. Soup is now ready to heat and garnish or chill. It freezes well up to 3 months.

Th␣␣ ␣␣ at Egg

. . .

Recipes for Yolks

Pat Kery and Pat Field

For Silvia love Pat Kery

St. Martin's Press • New York

Design by Laura Hammond Hough

Library of Congress Cataloging in Publication Data

Kery, Patricia Frantz.
    The separate egg.

    1. Cookery (Eggs)   I. Field, Pat.   II. Title.
TX745.K47   1985   641.6′754   85-12527
ISBN 0-312-71303-7 (pbk.)

First Edition
10 9 8 7 6 5 4 3 2 1

Contents

• • •

Note: The number of egg yolks needed in each recipe is indicated by the circled number in the margin.

Introduction and Acknowledgments

• • •

This book is dedicated to all those who have been struck with "guilt pains" when pouring old, greening yolks or cloudy whites down the drain. One day, after having a large dinner party, I watched 22 whites slip into the sink. It was just too much! So I went into action. I scrutinized my cookbooks for recipes using the yolk or white of the separated egg. And now the work is done for you. Use this book to preplan your dinner parties so the whites and yolks come out even. Or just enjoy the recipes—they are our favorites. *Bon appetit!*

I would like to thank a few people who helped make this book possible: Pat Baird, Cindy Branch, Walter Bonsall, Judith Caseley, Sylvie Erals, Michele Fairchild, Nita Frantz, Barbara Fultz, Gaby (owner of the Brasserie in Washington, D.C.), Peter Hoffman, Deborah Horan, Michele Keith, Charlotte Larrabee, Jacques Mallet, Lionel Martinez, Jamie Schler, Michael Schler, and Luis Tossas. Some soufflé recipes are courtesy of Irena Chalmers Cookbooks, Inc. And lastly, a special thank-you to Pat Field, who is wonderfully diligent, a great cook, and a lot of fun to write a book with.

—PAT KERY

Appetizers

• • •

Scallop Seviche
SERVES 6

O Y O L K

3/4 cup lemon juice
3/4 cup lime juice
1/4 cup olive oil
2 teaspoons salt
1/2 teaspoon minced garlic
Freshly ground white pepper to taste
2 pounds sea scallops, cut crosswise into 1/4-inch slices

2 fresh hot red peppers, seeded and chopped
1 pint cherry tomatoes, halved and seeded
1 red onion, chopped
1 green pepper, cored, seeded, and chopped
1/4 cup minced fresh coriander
1 egg yolk, lightly beaten
Boston lettuce

Mix together lemon juice, lime juice, oil, salt, garlic, and ground pepper in a shallow glass or ceramic bowl. Add scallops and red pepper. Cover and let marinate in refrigerator for 2 hours, or until scallops are opaque, stirring occasionally.

Add cherry tomatoes, onion, green pepper, coriander, and egg yolk. Mix well. Cover and chill for 1 hour longer.

To serve, line plates with Boston lettuce and top with seviche.

Crab-Cheese Dip

MAKES ABOUT 2½ CUPS

O
Y
O
L
K

1 can (10¾ ounces) cream of
  shrimp soup
1 package (8 ounces) cream
  cheese, softened
1 egg yolk, beaten
1½ tablespoons sherry

1 can (6 ounces) crabmeat,
  drained and flaked
Salt and freshly ground black
  pepper to taste
½ teaspoon dried dillweed

Mix together soup and cheese in saucepan and cook, stirring, over low heat until blended. Stir small amount of hot mixture into egg yolk in bowl. Return to hot mixture. Add sherry and cook, stirring constantly, until thickened. Stir in crabmeat, salt and pepper, and dillweed.

Serve hot with crackers or over toast points.

Quiche Lorraine

SERVES 6 TO 8

Pastry for 9-inch pie
4 slices bacon
1 cup thinly sliced onions
1 1/2 cups diced Gruyère or
   Swiss cheese
2 eggs, lightly beaten
2 egg yolks, lightly beaten

1 cup heavy cream
1 cup milk
1/2 teaspoon salt
1/4 teaspoon nutmeg
1/4 teaspoon freshly ground
   black pepper

Preheat oven to 450°F.

Line 9-inch pie plate with pastry and bake for 5 minutes. Maintain oven temperature.

Cook bacon until crisp, then crumble, drain, and set aside. Cook onions in bacon drippings until transparent.

Cover bottom of pastry shell evenly with cheese, bacon, and cooked onions. Combine remaining ingredients and pour over onions and cheese.

Bake in 450°F oven for 10 minutes, then reduce heat to 350°F and bake an additional 15 to 20 minutes, or until knife inserted in center comes out clean.

Hot Mushroom Caps

MAKES 36

36 large fresh mushrooms
(about 1 pound), wiped clean
and stemmed
1/2 cup butter
9 slices bread
1 package (12 ounces) cream
cheese

3 egg yolks
3 tablespoons freshly grated
Parmesan cheese
1 small garlic clove, peeled and
chopped

Preheat broiler.

Sauté mushroom caps, in the butter, until lightly browned.

Toast bread slices. Remove crusts and cut each slice into quarters. Arrange bread squares on broiler pan or cookie sheet. Place one mushroom cap, open side down, on each piece of toast.

In mixing bowl, whip cream cheese; add egg yolks, salt, and garlic. Beat until smooth. Spoon mixture over mushroom caps.

Broil 8 inches from heat until lightly browned.

NOTE: This appetizer is easily frozen.

Oysters Bienville

SERVES 4

BIENVILLE SAUCE

1/2 cup lightly salted butter
*1 cup finely chopped shallots or
  scallions*
*1/4 cup finely minced fresh
  parsley*
*1 1/2 teaspoons finely minced
  garlic*
1/2 cup all-purpose flour
1/2 cup heavy cream
1 1/2 cups milk

4 large egg yolks, well beaten
1/4 cup dry sherry
3/4 teaspoon salt
*1 teaspoon finely ground white
  pepper*
3 dashes cayenne pepper
*2/3 cup finely chopped fresh
  mushrooms*
*1/2 pound shrimp, boiled,
  peeled, and finely diced*

*2 dozen oysters on the half
  shell, drained*
4 pans rock salt

TOPPING (optional)

*1/2 cup freshly grated Romano
  cheese*
1/4 cup fine dry bread crumbs

1/2 teaspoon paprika
1/2 teaspoon salt

In large heavy saucepan, melt butter over low heat. Add shallots,
parsley, and garlic and cook, stirring frequently, about 10 minutes.

Gradually stir in flour and mix with a wooden spoon until smooth. Add cream and milk slowly, stirring constantly until mixture is quite smooth. Add egg yolks, sherry, salt, pepper, and cayenne, blending thoroughly. Continue cooking over low heat until mixture begins to thicken. Stir in mushrooms and cook for 2 minutes, then add shrimp and continue to cook over low heat for about 3 to 4 minutes, until sauce is quite thick. Remove from heat.

Spoon sauce into large shallow porcelain or glass dish, to a depth of 1½ to 2 inches. Let cool for a few minutes at room temperature, then cover with plastic wrap and refrigerate for at least 1½ hours.

Preheat oven to 500°F. Heat pans of rock salt in oven for 30 minutes.

Arrange oysters, on half shells, on top of rock salt. Spoon 1 heaping tablespoon of sauce evenly over each oyster. Prepare optional topping by mixing all ingredients in blender at high speed for a few seconds, then turning blender off; repeat several times. Sprinkle 1 level teaspoon of topping evenly over each sauced oyster. Bake 15 to 18 minutes, or until well browned on top.

Soups

• • •

Cream of Asparagus Soup

SERVES 4

3 tablespoons butter
2 small bunches asparagus,
   sliced, tips removed and
   reserved
1 bunch scallions, chopped
1 garlic clove, chopped
Few drops of lemon juice

Salt and freshly ground black
   pepper to taste
1/4 cup all-purpose flour
2 cups water
1/2 cup cream
1 egg yolk, lightly beaten

Melt butter in pan. Add sliced asparagus, scallions, garlic, lemon juice, salt, and pepper. Cook over low heat, stirring, until asparagus are very soft. Stir in flour; mix well. Pour in water and stir over medium heat until soup comes to a boil. Simmer, uncovered, for 10 minutes. Process until smooth in blender or food processor. Return to pan.

Boil reserved asparagus tips in salted water until tender. Drain and add to soup.

Mix together cream and egg yolk. Stir in 1 or 2 tablespoons hot soup. Return mixture gradually to soup. Heat thoroughly, taking care not to boil.

11

Almond Soup

SERVES 6

1/4 cup butter
1 cup blanched almonds,
    toasted and ground in food
    processor or blender
1/4 teaspoon salt
Pinch of freshly ground black
    pepper

1 can (13 3/4 ounces) condensed
    chicken broth
1 tablespoon cornstarch
1 egg yolk, lightly beaten
1 cup half-and-half or light
    cream
Toasted sliced almonds

Melt butter in saucepan over low heat. Add almonds, salt, and pepper and cook till butter browns lightly.

Mix together chicken broth and cornstarch; add to almond mixture. Simmer 10 minutes, stirring frequently.

Beat together egg yolk and half-and-half. Gradually add to broth, stirring constantly; do not allow to boil.

Serve hot or chilled, garnished with sliced almonds.

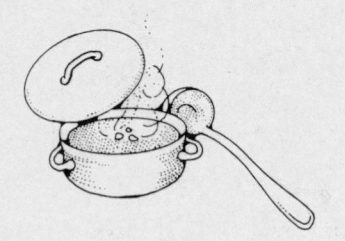

Cream of Chestnut Soup

SERVES 6 TO 8

¾ pound fresh chestnuts (see
    note on page 14)
4 tablespoons butter
1 parsnip, peeled and finely
    chopped
2 carrots, peeled and finely
    chopped
3 stalks celery, peeled and finely
    chopped

½ pound lean boneless veal,
    cut into ¼-inch cubes
5 cups water
1 teaspoon salt
¼ teaspoon freshly ground
    black pepper
½ cup heavy cream
2 egg yolks

Preheat oven to 350°F.

Wash chestnuts. Cut a gash in the side of each. Place nuts in a heavy pan, adding 1 teaspoon oil for each cup of nuts. Shake until nuts are coated with oil. Place pan in oven and heat until shells and skins can easily be removed, 5 to 8 minutes. Remove shells and skins with a sharp knife. Place chestnuts in a large saucepan, cover with boiling salted water, and cook over low heat for 15 to 20 minutes, until tender when tested with a toothpick. Drain and purée in a blender.

Melt butter in a heavy soup kettle. Add vegetables and meat and sauté until browned, about 10 minutes. Add water, salt, and pepper and cook, uncovered, over low heat for about 10 minutes, to heat through. Mix in puréed chestnuts and simmer for another 5 minutes.

Mix cream with egg yolks, then whisk into soup. Taste for seasoning. Serve hot.

NOTE: Canned chestnuts can be substituted for the puréed fresh.

Leek and Potato Soup

SERVES 4 TO 6

2 YOLKS

4 tablespoons butter
4 large potatoes, peeled and
thinly sliced
2 medium bunches leeks,
cleaned thoroughly and
shredded
1 1/2 cups water

Salt and freshly ground black
pepper to taste
1/2 teaspoon Dijon mustard
1 1/2 cups milk
2 egg yolks
1/2 cup heavy cream
Chopped fresh parsley or chives
Croutons (optional)

Melt butter in saucepan. Add potatoes and leeks (reserve 1 cup shredded leeks). Add 1/2 cup of the water, salt, pepper, and mustard. Cover and cook over low heat until vegetables are soft. Add milk and remaining 1 cup water; stir until soup comes to a boil. Remove from heat; let cool slightly. Purée in blender.

Combine yolks and cream in saucepan. Heat over low flame, taking care not to boil. Stir in puréed soup mixture.

Cover reserved leeks with water in second saucepan; bring to a boil. Drain and add to soup. Sprinkle with parsley or chives and croutons; serve immediately.

Watercress Soup

SERVES 6

3 large boiling potatoes, peeled
  and quartered
1 large onion, quartered
6 cups chicken stock or broth
2 bunches watercress, trimmed,
  rinsed, and dried

Salt and freshly ground black
  pepper to taste
3 egg yolks
1/2 cup heavy cream
Watercress sprigs

Place potatoes and onion in a saucepan, cover with the chicken stock or broth, and bring liquid to a boil. Reduce heat and simmer, uncovered, for 20 minutes, or until potatoes are tender.

Place watercress in a blender or food processor and process for 20 seconds. Remove to a bowl. Transfer potatoes and onion to blender or food processor; reserve stock. Add 3 tablespoons of stock and process for 15 seconds to purée.

Remove purée to a heavy kettle. Add watercress and remaining stock. Bring soup to a boil, stirring constantly. Add salt and pepper; reduce heat to very low. Place egg yolks in the blender or food processor and, with motor running, slowly add cream. Continue processing for 30 seconds. Add 2 tablespoons of soup to yolk mixture; blend. Slowly add yolk mixture to soup, stirring constantly. Heat soup for 3 to 4 minutes to thicken it slightly; take care not to let soup boil or eggs will scramble. Garnish with watercress sprigs.

Cindy's Sorrel Soup

SERVES 6

**4
Y
O
L
K
S**

2 medium boiling potatoes,
  washed, peeled, and
  quartered
4 cups chicken stock or broth
4 tablespoons butter
1/2 cup chopped onions
1 pound sorrel, washed, stems
  removed, and chopped or
  finely shredded

4 egg yolks
1 cup light cream
Salt and freshly ground pepper
  to taste
Crème fraîche or sour cream
  (optional)

Place potatoes in saucepan and cover with chicken stock. Bring to boil and simmer until potatoes can be pierced with fork, about 15 minutes. With slotted spoon, transfer potato quarters to blender or food processor; reserve stock in saucepan. Process potatoes until puréed. Return to stock and stir until well mixed.

Melt butter in second saucepan and sauté onion until soft and transparent. Add sorrel and cook until greens are limp. Add mixture to stock and stir well.

Place egg yolks in blender or food processor; process for 2 seconds. With motor running, slowly add cream; process until frothy. Add 2 tablespoons of soup to yolk mixture; blend. Gradually add yolk mixture to soup. Let simmer for 5 minutes, stirring constantly. Season with salt and pepper.

Serve hot or chilled, topped, if desired with crème fraîche or sour cream.

Entrées

• • •

Stuffed Pork Chops
SERVES 8

1 cup chopped walnuts or
   pecans
2 cups fresh bread crumbs
Salt and freshly ground black
   pepper to taste
1 small onion, chopped
Chopped fresh parsley to taste
1 tablespoon butter
1 egg yolk, beaten

1 apple, cored and chopped
1/4 cup heavy cream
1 teaspoon poultry seasoning
Cayenne pepper to taste
8 thick pork chops, each with a
   pocket
All-purpose flour
Vegetable oil
1/4 cup water (optional)

Preheat oven to 350°F. Mix nuts and crumbs in bowl. Season with salt and pepper. Sauté onion and parsley in butter in small skillet until onion is tender. Remove from heat and add to nut mixture along with egg yolk and apple. Stir in cream and poultry seasoning.

Stuff pockets of pork chops with mixture. Season well with cayenne, black pepper, and salt. Dredge chops lightly in flour and brown well in a lightly oiled heavy skillet. Transfer chops, with any resulting juices, to a heavy pan and bake for 1 1/2 hours. Add 1/4 cup of water to pan while baking, if necessary. Use drippings to make gravy, if desired.

Chicken Tarragon
SERVES 4

O
Y
O
L
K

4 whole chicken breasts, split,
   skinned, and boned
11 tablespoons butter
Salt and freshly ground black
   pepper to taste
1/4 cup all-purpose flour
Cayenne pepper to taste

2 cups chicken stock or broth
2 tablespoons heavy cream
3 tablespoons dried tarragon
1 egg yolk
1 tablespoon milk
1 1/2 cups hot, cooked rice
Paprika

Pound chicken breasts flat.

Melt 6 tablespoons of the butter in large skillet. Add chicken and turn to coat with the butter. Sprinkle with salt and pepper. Cook, covered, over low heat for 10 to 15 minutes or until chicken is tender, turning once.

Meanwhile, melt 3 tablespoons of the butter in a saucepan. Stir in flour and salt and cayenne pepper to taste. Blend well. Gradually add chicken stock, stirring constantly until mixture comes to a boil. Add remaining 2 tablespoons butter; gradually blend in cream. Simmer about 5 minutes, stirring constantly. Add tarragon.

Beat milk and egg yolk. Add to the sauce.

To serve, place chicken breasts on top of rice. Pour sauce over the chicken, sprinkle with paprika, and serve immediately.

Coquilles St. Jacques

4 SERVINGS

8 tablespoons butter
1/4 cup all-purpose flour
1 cup fish stock or bottled clam
 juice
1/2 cup dry white wine
2 egg yolks
1 cup heavy cream
2 teaspoons Dijon mustard
3 cups scallops, rinsed and
 drained

1/2 pound fresh mushrooms,
 wiped clean and sliced
Salt and freshly ground black
 pepper to taste
2 garlic cloves, minced
1/2 cup minced shallots
1/2 cup freshly grated Parmesan
 or Swiss cheese
1 tablespoon paprika

Preheat oven to 350°F.

Melt 6 tablespoons of the butter in a saucepan; add flour and mix well. Gradually stir in fish stock and wine until sauce is smooth and has thickened somewhat. Whisk yolks thoroughly in bowl; add cream and continue to whisk. When blended, add to wine mixture. Stir in mustard, then scallops. Season to taste. Sauté garlic, mushrooms, and shallots in remaining 2 tablespoons butter in small skillet until shallots are tender. Add to scallop mixture and cook together a few minutes.

Spoon mixture into scallop shells or individual ramekins. Mix cheese and paprika; sprinkle over shells. Dot with butter and bake until browned, 5 to 10 minutes. Serve immediately.

Trout Marguery

SERVES 4

2 small to medium-size
  speckled trout fillets

POACHING LIQUID

2¹/2 cups water
¹/4 cup dry white wine
1 tablespoon butter
1 teaspoon salt

3 whole peppercorns
1 bay leaf, broken in half
¹/8 teaspoon dried thyme
1 lemon slice (¹/4 inch thick)

MARGUERY SAUCE

¹/2 cup butter
¹/4 cup all-purpose flour
2¹/2 cups hot liquid (the
  strained poaching liquid plus
  enough boiling water to make
  2¹/2 cups)

2 egg yolks, lightly beaten
1 tablespoon lemon juice
¹/4 teaspoon salt
1 pound shrimp, boiled and
  peeled
¹/2 cup sliced fresh mushrooms

Preheat oven to 175°F.

To poach trout fillets, combine all ingredients for poaching liquid in large heavy skillet or sauté pan. Bring to boil over high heat, then reduce heat so liquid is just at simmer. Add trout and cook at low simmer 5 to 6 minutes. (Fish will flake easily when pricked with fork if done; do not overcook.) Remove fish from liquid with slotted spatula, letting excess liquid drain off. Place fish on platter and set in preheated oven to keep warm. Strain and reserve poaching liquid.

In heavy 2- to 3-quart saucepan, melt 3 tablespoons butter over low heat. Add flour and stir until smooth; do not allow to brown. Gradually add hot liquid, stirring constantly with whisk or spoon to smoothen. Cook over low heat until thickened, about 5 to 7 minutes, stirring constantly.

Remove pan from heat. Add egg yolks, lemon juice, and salt; blend well with whisk.

In another small saucepan, over low heat, melt remaining butter.

Return large saucepan to low heat and slowly add melted butter; blend well. Add shrimp and mushrooms. Cook over very low heat, stirring gently, until shrimp and mushrooms are heated through (about 4 to 6 minutes). Do not allow sauce to boil.

To serve, place fish on plates and top with sauce.

Filet Mignon Wellington

SERVES 2

HERB PASTRY

2 cups all-purpose flour

4 tablespoons butter, cut in
small pieces

1 egg yolk

1 teaspoon salt

2 teaspoons dried tarragon

2 tablespoons lemon juice

1/2 cup ice water

FILET

2 beef tenderloins (6 ounces
each)

Salt and freshly ground pepper

2 egg yolks, lightly beaten

2 ounces liver pâté

First make herb pastry. In the workbowl of a food processor or mixer, place flour, butter, egg yolk, salt, and tarragon. Process for several minutes until ingredients are well blended.

Add lemon juice to ice water and, with mixer or food processor running, pour the liquid in a stream into workbowl. Continue processing until mixture resembles coarse meal.

Remove dough from processor and shape it into a ball. Dust dough with flour, wrap in wax paper, and refrigerate for at least 1 hour.

Preheat broiler.

Roll out the pastry to thickness of 1/4 inch, flouring generously as you roll. Cut out 2 round pieces about the size of a silver dollar and 2 pieces about 6 inches in diameter.

Salt and pepper filets to taste and broil quickly on both sides, keeping meat rare. Let filets cool for 15 minutes.

Meanwhile, preheat oven to 400°F.

Place each cooled filet on a 6-inch piece of dough; brush dough around filet with egg yolk. Place 1 teaspoon of pâté on each filet and wrap filet in dough. Brush egg yolk over outside of each pastry-wrapped filet and seal each with a small dough round. Brush again with egg yolk.

Bake for 15 minutes, or until pastry is golden brown.

NOTE: For an extra rich recipe, sauté 4 sliced fresh mushrooms in a little butter until soft. In a separate skillet, cook 4 slices bacon until crisp and drain. Crumble bacon into small pieces and combine with mushrooms and butter. Pat half into a layer on top of each pâté layer and seal as directed above.

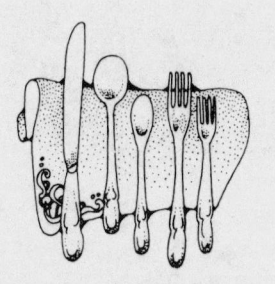

Eggs Royale
SERVES 4

3 YOLKS

1 pound chicken livers, finely
  chopped
1/3 cup finely chopped shallots
3 egg yolks

8 eggs
1 cup Hollandaise Sauce (see
  Yolks, page 36)

Preheat oven to 375°F.

Mix chicken livers, shallots, and egg yolks. Place in buttered loaf pan set in larger pan of water. Bake until set, 25 to 30 minutes. Remove pan from oven; reduce oven temperature to 350°F.

Unmold pâté and slice like bread (at least 8 slices). Place 2 slices of sliced pâté in each of 4 ramekins. Break 2 raw eggs into each ramekin. Bake for about 4 minutes, depending on desired softness of eggs. Remove from oven and top with sauce. Serve immediately.

Renee's Steak Tartar

SERVES 4

4 egg yolks
2 pounds very lean ground
   sirloin
3 shallots or 1 large onion,
   minced
2 garlic cloves, crushed
6 anchovy fillets (optional),
   mashed
2 tablespoons capers
7 tablespoons olive oil

2 teaspoons Dijon mustard
1 teaspoon Worcestershire
   sauce
1/4 cup brandy
5 teaspoons chopped fresh
   parsley
4 teaspoons lemon juice
2 teaspoons salt
1 teaspoon freshly ground black
   pepper

Combine all ingredients and mix well. This dish is traditionally prepared at the table. Serve with cocktail breads or toasts.

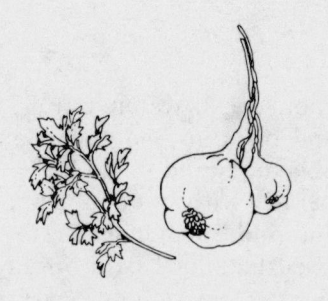

Blanquette de Veau

SERVES 4

5 YOLKS

1 pound large fresh
   mushrooms, wiped clean,
   caps cut into $1/8$-inch pieces,
   and stems reserved
$3/4$ cup water
1 tablespoon butter
Salt
2 pounds boneless veal
   shoulder, trimmed and cut
   into 1- to $1^1/2$-inch cubes
Freshly ground black pepper
   to taste
1 cup dry white wine
2 carrots
2 leeks, with 2 inches of green,
   washed and quartered

$1/2$ medium onion
3 to 4 sprigs fresh tarragon
3 sprigs fresh thyme
1 small celery stalk with leaves,
   coarsely chopped
1 bay leaf
2 to 3 garlic cloves, unpeeled
1 pound baby carrots, peeled, or
   4 carrots, peeled, halved
   lengthwise, and cut into
   thirds
1 cup heavy cream
5 egg yolks

Combine mushroom caps, water, butter, and salt in medium saucepan. Cover and bring to boil over high heat. Remove from heat and drain, reserving liquid.

Sprinkle veal liberally with salt and pepper. Transfer to 6-quart saucepan. Add wine and enough water to cover. Bring to boil, skimming foam off surface for first 5 minutes. Tie carrots, leeks, onions, tarragon, thyme, celery, and bay leaf in cheesecloth and

add to saucepan with reserved mushroom stems and unpeeled garlic. Reduce heat, cover, and simmer until veal is tender, about 1 hour.

Meanwhile, in medium saucepan, blanch baby carrots in boiling water until tender, about 3 minutes. Drain and immediately plunge into ice water to stop cooking process. Drain.

Transfer meat to platter. Discard cheesecloth bag.

Increase heat to medium and reduce stock by one-third. Strain stock into bowl, pressing vegetables with back of wooden spoon to extract maximum amount of liquid. Return stock to saucepan. Add reserved mushroom liquid and ½ cup of the cream. Cook over medium heat until reduced by another third. Season with salt and pepper. (Sauce can be prepared ahead to this point, covered, and refrigerated up to 2 days. Rewarm slowly over low heat before serving.)

Beat egg yolks with remaining ½ cup cream in medium bowl. Whisk about 3 tablespoons warm sauce into yolk mixture, then transfer mixture to sauce. Cook over medium heat, stirring constantly, until sauce coats spoon; do not allow to boil.

Return meat, carrots, and mushrooms to pan, stirring into sauce. Cook until heated through. Serve with rice or pasta.

Cold and Mild
Dressings

• • •

Creamy Salad Dressing
MAKES ABOUT ¾ CUP

1 teaspoon beaten egg yolk
2 teaspoons Dijon mustard
Dash or two of Tabasco
½ teaspoon finely chopped garlic

Salt and freshly ground black pepper to taste
1 teaspoon vinegar
½ cup olive oil or vegetable oil
1 teaspoon lemon juice
1 teaspoon heavy cream

Mix together egg yolk and mustard. Add Tabasco, garlic, salt and pepper, and vinegar. Beat vigorously with whisk. Gradually add oil, continuing to beat with whisk. Whisk until thickened and well blended. Add lemon juice. Beat in heavy cream. Taste and adjust seasoning if necessary.

Caesar Salad

SERVES 4

1 head romaine lettuce, washed
and patted dry
2 to 3 garlic cloves
1 teaspoon salt
1/2 cup light olive oil
1 cup French bread cubes
1 small can anchovy fillets
(optional)
1/4 teaspoon dry mustard

1/4 teaspoon freshly ground
black pepper
2 teaspoons Worcestershire
sauce
1 egg yolk
1/4 cup Gorgonzola or blue
cheese, crumbled
2 tablespoons freshly grated
Parmesan or Romano cheese
Juice of 1/2 lemon

Crush 1 to 2 garlic cloves, setting remaining clove aside for later
use. Mash crushed garlic with salt into paste, mix with olive oil in
jar, and let stand at least 2 hours in refrigerator.

Sauté bread cubes in small pan, using enough garlic-oil mixture
just to cover bottom of pan. Remove when well browned and set
aside.

Add anchovies, mustard, pepper, and Worcestershire sauce to jar
of garlic-oil mixture; shake well.

Prepare salad bowl by rubbing with remaining garlic clove,
halved. Tear lettuce into pieces and place in bowl. Shake dressing,
pour over greens, and add cheeses. Toss salad. Add egg yolk to
salad, along with lemon juice; toss again. Add sautéed bread
cubes, toss, and serve at once.

❶ Sherri's Herb-Buttermilk Dressing

MAKES ABOUT 2 CUPS

Y
O
L
K

1 egg
1 egg yolk
1 tablespoon white vinegar
2 teaspoons Dijon mustard
1 small garlic clove, crushed
³/₄ teaspoon salt
³/₄ teaspoon dried dillweed
¹/₂ teaspoon dried thyme

¹/₂ teaspoon dried marjoram
¹/₂ teaspoon dried basil
¹/₂ teaspoon dried chervil
¹/₂ cup vegetable or almond oil
1 cup buttermilk
Freshly ground white pepper to
taste

Place eggs and egg yolk, vinegar, mustard, garlic, salt, and herbs in food processor or blender. Process briefly. With motor running, gradually add oil and buttermilk. Add pepper to taste.

30

Sauces

• • •

Velouté Sauce

MAKES ABOUT 1 1/4 CUPS

Use on chicken or veal dishes.

1 egg yolk
1 1/2 tablespoons heavy cream
1 tablespoon butter

1 tablespoon all-purpose flour
1 cup chicken broth

Stir together egg yolk and cream in a mixing bowl. Set aside.

Melt the butter in a saucepan. Remove from heat and whisk in flour. Over medium heat, add chicken broth, stirring constantly.

Transfer about 3 tablespoons of the hot sauce to yolk and cream mixture; stir together. Return this to remaining hot sauce, taking care not to let sauce boil after egg yolk and cream have been added. Stir together over low heat until thickened and smooth.

1 EGG YOLK

Mushroom Wine Sauce

MAKES ABOUT 2½ CUPS

Use on steak, filet mignon, pot roast, noodles, meat loaf, or poultry.

¼ cup sliced fresh mushrooms
3 tablespoons butter
2 tablespoons all-purpose flour
1 cup chicken stock
½ cup dry white wine
½ teaspoon dried tarragon

Salt and freshly ground black
  pepper to taste
½ cup half-and-half
1 egg yolk

Sauté mushrooms in 1 tablespoon of the butter in a small skillet; set aside.

Melt remaining 2 tablespoons butter in a saucepan; stir in flour. Cook, stirring constantly, for 1 minute. Add chicken stock, wine, tarragon, and salt and pepper. Simmer for several minutes. Add mushrooms and simmer for 5 minutes longer; remove from heat.

Beat cream and egg yolk to blend; stir gradually into mushroom mixture. Cook, stirring constantly, until mixture is hot, do not allow to boil. Serve hot.

Béarnaise Sauce

MAKES ABOUT 3/4 CUP

Use on steaks, hamburgers, poached eggs, and artichokes.

1 tablespoon sliced scallions
2 tablespoons red wine vinegar
1/2 teaspoon freshly ground
  black pepper
3 tablespoons chopped fresh
  tarragon or 1 1/2 teaspoons
  dried

2 egg yolks
1 tablespoon water
1 tablespoon cold butter
1 cup butter, melted
Salt to taste

Combine the scallions, vinegar, pepper, and 2 tablespoons fresh (or 1 teaspoon dried) tarragon in a saucepan. Cook over low heat until vinegar has evaporated. Remove from heat; let mixture cool briefly.

Add yolks and water to mixture in saucepan, beating vigorously with a whisk. Place over low heat and continue beating rapidly until yolks start to thicken; take care that they do not overheat, or they will scramble. Beat in cold butter and remove from heat.

Slowly add melted butter to yolk mixture, beating rapidly with the whisk. Continue beating until all the butter has been added. Add salt; beat in remaining tarragon.

Mayonnaise

MAKES ABOUT 2 CUPS

Use on salads, sandwiches, and cold meats and chicken.

2 egg yolks, at room
   temperature
1 whole egg
2 tablespoons lemon juice
1 teaspoon salt

1 teaspoon Dijon mustard
   (optional)
3/4 cup vegetable oil
3/4 cup virgin olive oil
1/2 teaspoon freshly ground
   black pepper

Place egg yolks, egg, lemon juice, salt, and mustard in blender or
food processor; process 5 seconds. With motor running, gradually
add oils; process until well blended and thickened. Adjust seasoning if necessary.

VARIATIONS

1. For a thicker sauce, eliminate whole egg (for fish mousses,
cold meats, chicken).

2. For a lighter mayonnaise, substitute white vinegar for vegetable oil.

3. *Herbed Mayonnaise:* Eliminate whole egg. Add 1/2 cup tightly
packed combination of parsley leaves, chevril, watercress, and
spinach that have been blanched in boiling water for 2 minutes,
drained, and puréed.

Quick Hollandaise Sauce

Use on eggs Benedict, asparagus, broccoli, cauliflower, and fish.

3 egg yolks
2 tablespoons lemon juice
1/4 teaspoon salt
2 dashes Tabasco

1/4 teaspoon dry mustard
1/8 teaspoon cayenne pepper
1/2 cup butter, melted and hot

Combine egg yolks, lemon juice, salt, Tabasco, mustard, and cayenne in a blender. Cover blender and switch on and off several times. Remove central portion of cover, or keep blender partially covered, and switch to high speed; add hot butter in a slow, steady stream, until just blended and thickened. Serve immediately, or keep warm by placing blender container in a pan of hot water.

Mustard Sauce

MAKES ABOUT 2 CUPS

4 YOLKS

Use on ham, savory crêpes, corned beef, sausage, fish, shellfish, and spinach.

4 egg yolks, lightly beaten
1 teaspoon salt
1/8 teaspoon freshly ground
   white pepper
4 teaspoons vinegar

2 cups vegetable oil
1 tablespoon lemon juice
1/4 cup prepared mustard
2 tablespoons honey

Beat together egg yolks, salt, white pepper, and vinegar. Pour oil very slowly into eggs, beating continuously at medium speed. Add lemon juice, mustard, and honey; blend well.

Hollandaise Sauce

MAKES ABOUT 1 1/4 CUPS

4 YOLKS

Use on eggs Benedict, asparagus, broccoli, cauliflower, and fish.

4 egg yolks, beaten
2 tablespoons lemon juice
1 cup butter, melted
1/4 teaspoon salt

Freshly ground black pepper to
   taste
Dash of cayenne (optional)

Add lemon juice to egg yolks in top of double boiler. Cook very slowly over simmering water; do not allow to boil. Gradually add melted butter, stirring constantly with a wooden spoon. Add seasonings and continue to cook, stirring constantly, until thickened.

• • •

Marquise au Chocolat
SERVES 8

O
Y
O
L
K

8 ounces semisweet chocolate,
  cut into small pieces
1 cup plus 2 tablespoons
  confectioners sugar
3/4 cup unsalted butter, cut into
  1/2-inch pats
6 egg yolks

3/4 cup unsweetened cocoa
  powder
5 egg whites
Dash of salt
Dash of cream of tartar
3/4 cup heavy cream

Melt chocolate in a heatproof bowl set over simmering water.
Maintain simmer. Add sugar and mix well. Stir in butter, one piece
at a time, and blend well. Remove bowl from over water and add
egg yolks one at a time, mixing well after each addition. Beat in
cocoa. Let cool 5 minutes, stirring frequently.

Beat egg whites with salt and cream of tartar until stiff peaks
form. Gently stir one third of whites into chocolate mixture, then
fold remaining whites into chocolate mixture; do not beat. Whip
cream to soft peaks. Carefully fold whipped cream into chocolate

37

mixture until well blended. Pour into 9 x 5-inch glass loaf pan or 1½-quart glass mold (do not use metal). Chill at least 12 hours.

Just before serving, moisten kitchen towel with hot water. Wrap towel around mold and invert onto platter. Serve immediately. Serve with Marquise Sauce (see below) or Crème Anglaise (see Yolks, page 43).

Marquise Sauce
MAKES ABOUT 4 CUPS

2
Y
O
L
K
S

1 cup granulated sugar
3 cups heavy cream
2 egg yolks, beaten

3 tablespoons Kahlúa liqueur
½ cup very strongly brewed
  espresso coffee

Melt sugar in a heavy-bottomed skillet without stirring, swirling pan so that sugar moves about as it melts. Continue to swirl until sugar becomes caramel-colored. Carefully and very slowly pour in heavy cream. Cook over low heat for 15 minutes.

Let saucepan stand in a cold place until just warm. Add yolks, along with Kahlúa and coffee; mix all together well. Cool 1 to 2 hours.

Sablés (Cookies)

¾ cup unsalted butter, softened
⅔ cup granulated sugar

2 egg yolks
2 cups all-purpose flour

Preheat oven to 350°F.

Cream together butter and sugar with an electric mixer or in a food processor. Add egg yolks and mix for 30 seconds. Add half the flour and mix until smooth. Add remaining flour and mix until well blended. Wrap cookie dough in plastic wrap and chill until very cold.

Place one-third of the dough at a time on a well-floured board. (Keep remainder of dough chilled until ready for use.) Roll dough to ⅛-inch thickness. Cut into desired shapes with cookie cutters or a 2-inch biscuit cutter. Transfer to a buttered baking sheet. Chill cut cookies until all the dough has been used.

Sprinkle cookies lightly with sugar (colored crystal sugar may be used). Bake 8 to 10 minutes, until cookies are pale golden in color. Remove to a rack and cool.

Floating Island

SERVES 6

2 Y O L K S

2¼ cups milk
3 egg whites
1 cup granulated sugar

5 egg yolks
2 teaspoons vanilla

Bring milk to simmer in skillet over moderately low heat.

Beat egg whites with ⅓ cup of the sugar until stiff and shiny. Make "island" by scooping portion of meringue onto one spoon and placing other spoon gently on top to shape. Slide meringue into simmering milk, three or four at a time. Poach for 1 to 2 minutes on each side. Remove to paper toweling to drain.

Beat egg yolks until thick and pale, slowly adding remaining sugar. Gradually add simmering milk in which "islands" were poached.

Transfer to heavy-bottomed pan and cook over low heat, stirring constantly, until mixture thickens; do not allow to boil. Pour into mixing bowl and stir in vanilla; let cool, closely covered with plastic wrap or wax paper to prevent a skin from forming.

Put cooled custard in shallow bowl and arrange "islands" on top. Chill well before serving.

Zabaglione

MAKES ABOUT 1 CUP

3 egg yolks
6 tablespoons granulated sugar
1/2 cup Marsala wine

1/2 teaspoon lemon juice
Toasted almonds (optional)

In top of double boiler, beat together egg yolks and sugar until light. Beat in wine and lemon juice. Place over simmering water and continue to beat on medium speed until mixture thickens to a custardy consistency, about 5 minutes. Remove from heat.

Serve warm in large wine glasses. May be sprinkled with toasted almonds.

Country Apple Nut Cake with Sauce Campagne

CAKE

2 cups granulated sugar
2 eggs
1 1/2 cups corn oil
3 cups peeled, diced apples
3 cups all-purpose flour

1/2 teaspoon salt
1 teaspoon baking soda
1 teaspoon ground cinnamon
2 teaspoons vanilla
1 cup chopped nuts

Preheat oven to 300°F. Grease and flour a sheet cake pan.

Cream together sugar, eggs, and oil. Add apples.

Sift together dry ingredients. Add to apple mixture. Blend in vanilla and nuts. Pour batter into prepared pan and bake for 45 to 50 minutes.

SAUCE CAMPAGNE

1/3 cup butter
1 cup sifted confectioners sugar
*3 tablespoons brandy or orange
liqueur*

3 egg yolks
*1 cup half-and-half, at room
temperature*

Meanwhile, make Sauce Campagne. Cream butter until soft in top of double boiler (not over heat). Add confectioners sugar and beat until creamy. Place over simmering water and slowly add brandy, continuing to beat. Beat in egg yolks, one at a time. Add cream, stirring constantly. Cook until slightly thickened.

Serve the cake warm, topped with the warm sauce.

NOTE: Sauce may be prepared in advance, refrigerated, and reheated in top of double boiler.

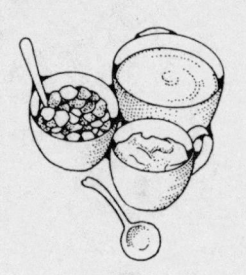

Pat Baird's Cheesecake

3
Y
O
L
K
S

3 packages (8 ounces each)
  cream cheese
2 cups sour cream
6 egg yolks
1 tablespoon vanilla

1 1/2 teaspoons lemon juice
1 cup granulated sugar
3 tablespoons all-purpose flour
3 egg whites, beaten to soft
  peaks

Preheat oven to 300°F.

Cream the cream cheese until soft; add 1 cup of the sour cream, the egg yolks, vanilla, and lemon juice and mix well. Add sugar and flour to mixture; fold in egg whites. Pour mixture into an 8- or 9-inch pan and bake for 1 hour.

Remove cake from oven and cool slightly. Spread remaining 1 cup sour cream over top. Chill 24 hours before serving.

Crème Anglaise

MAKES ABOUT 2 CUPS

4
Y
O
L
K
S

1 1/3 cups milk
1 vanilla bean, split lengthwise

4 egg yolks
1/3 cup granulated sugar

Scald milk with vanilla bean and set aside.

In double boiler, off heat, whisk yolks and sugar until lemon colored. Warm yolk mixture over simmering water, stirring con-

43

tinuously with a wooden spoon. Pour in milk and vanilla bean. Continue to stir until thick, about 20 minutes. Strain and cool in pan in a bowl of ice, stirring from time to time. When cool, cover and refrigerate.

Flan

SERVES 5

4 YOLKS

8 tablespoons granulated sugar
1 teaspoon water
2 cups milk

4 egg yolks, beaten
$^1/_2$ teaspoon vanilla

Preheat oven to 325°F.

Combine 6 tablespoons of the sugar and water in baking dish. Heat over low heat, stirring periodically, until sugar caramelizes. Remove from heat and let cool.

Mix together milk, egg yolks, vanilla, and remaining 2 tablespoons sugar. Pour into caramelized mixture. Place dish in large pan filled with water to level of $^1/_2$ inch. Bake 1 hour.

Remove flan from oven and chill.

To serve, unmold by inverting on platter so caramel is on top.

Dobos Torte (Seven-Layer Cake with Butter-Cream Frosting)

CAKE

5 eggs, separated (use large, not
   jumbo eggs)
1 tablespoon ice water
Pinch of salt

$^1/_2$ cup plus $^1/_3$ cup granulated
   sugar
$^1/_2$ cup pastry flour

Preheat oven to 375°F. Whip egg whites with ice water and a pinch of salt till stiff. Add yolks one at a time, beating for 1 minute after each addition. Add the $^1/_2$ cup sugar, spoon by spoon, beating all the time. (If you are using an electric mixer, turn down to lowest speed.) Add flour, little by little, making sure that it is completely blended into egg mixture.

Pour batter evenly into 7 cake pans. Tap sides a few times to level batter. Bake for 10 to 12 minutes, until golden brown.

Turn layers out on racks to cool, covering with kitchen towels or fresh wax paper in order to retain some of the moisture.

BUTTER-CREAM FROSTING
MAKES ABOUT 2$^3/_4$ CUPS

1 cup granulated sugar
$^1/_2$ cup cold water
$^1/_2$ teaspoon white corn syrup
Pinch of salt

5 egg yolks
1 teaspoon vanilla
1$^1/_4$ cups butter

In a saucepan, cook sugar, water, and corn syrup to 242°F on a candy thermometer, or until a few drops in water make a firm-soft ball.

While this boils, add salt to yolks in a small mixing bowl. Start to beat when syrup reaches 230°F. Beat until light and fluffy.

Gradually pour hot syrup into yolks while continuing to beat. Add vanilla. Continue to beat frosting until it has cooled somewhat.

Cream the butter and blend into the cooled frosting. Spread over cake or use as a filling. If frosting seems soft, refrigerate and the butter will firm it.

Spread the frosting on 6 layers. Put the layers together and frost the sides. Put rest of the frosting in a pastry bag fitted with a no. 6 tube.

Melt the 1/3 cup sugar in a heavy skillet over very low heat; stir it with a buttered spoon as it cooks. The sugar at first will look like dirty snow; then it will dissolve into a shiny, walnut-colored liquid. Immediately remove from the heat and spoon caramel directly from skillet pan onto remaining cake layer. Score it to intended portion sizes with tip of a buttered knife. (You must work fast because caramel will harden in less than a minute. Be careful not to touch the sugar with your hands.) When caramel is cool, put top layer on top of the filled layers. Pipe a decorative border of frosting around top edge of torte. Cool torte in the refrigerator at least 24 hours; it will keep in the refrigerator as long as 10 days.

To serve, slice the torte with a knife dipped into hot water.

Rice Pudding

SERVES 6

3 tablespoons converted rice
1/2 cup water
1/4 cup raisins
2 tablespoons dark rum
(optional)

3 cups heavy cream
3/4 cup granulated sugar
6 egg yolks
1/2 tablespoon vanilla
Nutmeg

Combine rice and water in a small saucepan. Bring to a boil; reduce heat and simmer 12 to 15 minutes. Remove from heat, cover, and let stand for 1 hour.

Drain any remaining liquid from rice. Add raisins and optional rum to rice and let stand an additional 1 to 3 hours at room temperature.

Preheat oven to 325°F. Place 2 level teaspoons of the rice mixture in each of six 6-ounce custard cups.

Mix cream and sugar together in a large saucepan. Heat, stirring constantly, until just below boiling point.

Gently beat egg yolks in a large mixing bowl. Add cream and sugar mixture a little at a time, mixing gently. Blend in vanilla. Pour the mixture over rice in custard cups. Sprinkle with nutmeg.

Place custard cups in a pan of hot water (the water should come halfway up sides of cups) and bake until a knife inserted in center of cups comes out clean, about 1 1/4 hours. Serve cold or at room temperature.

Gaby's Crème Brûlée

SERVES 6 to 8

6 EGG YOLKS

6 egg yolks
1 cup granulated sugar
1 egg

1 quart heavy cream
2 teaspoons vanilla
Brown sugar

Preheat oven to 275°F.

Beat together egg yolks and sugar. Add egg and beat again. Stir in heavy cream and vanilla. Pour into shallow baking dish; set in larger pan containing hot water. Place in oven and bake for 2½ hours.

Remove from oven and set in refrigerator to cool.

Meanwhile, heat broiler.

Generously sift brown sugar over surface of cooled crème. Place under broiler until sugar is caramelized. Let stand for 1 hour before serving.